USBORNE

# Classic
# Bible Stories
## for Little
# Children

Retold by Louie Stowell

Illustrated by Norman Young

Designed by Nelupa Hussain

# Contents

# Noah's Ark

There was once a man named Noah. He had a wife and three sons. Each son had a wife.

They were a very happy, busy, noisy family.

Noah was a farmer. He and his family worked hard in the fields all day long.

They cared for their animals kindly.

7

One day, God spoke to Noah.

"The people of earth are growing very wicked.
I'm going to send a flood to destroy them."

"You must build a gigantic ark and save
two of every animal from the flood."

God showed Noah how to build the boat.

Noah and his sons began to build the ark.

They hammered tough wood and wove bendy reeds together.

10

They covered the roof
with bundles of straw.

They slapped dark tar all over the ark, to keep the water out.

Finally, the ark was ready. Noah and his family loaded the boat with food and fresh, clean water.

Then the animals came – two by two.
"There's room for all of you," said Noah.

The animals hopped and scurried and slithered and waddled and jumped on board the ark.

There were pandas and penguins, mice and snakes, giraffes and lions and every other kind of animal.

When they were all on board...

... it began to rain

...and rain

...and rain

...and rain.

It rained for forty days
and forty nights.

Everyone inside was safe.
But the rest of the world
drowned in the flood.

One day, the rain stopped and the sky grew bright.
Soon, the tops of the mountains peeked through the waves.

Noah sent a raven to search for somewhere for them all to live. It flew for miles and miles.

But it couldn't find a new home anywhere.

As the days passed, the waters fell further.

Later, Noah
sent a dove to
search for land.

When it came back, it had an olive branch in its beak.

"That means the flood is over at last," said Noah. "Things are green and growing again."

When the land was properly dry, God opened the doors of the ark. The sun streamed in.

The animals scampered and waddled and crawled out of the ark. Noah's family rushed into the sunshine.

God spoke to them all. "Go wherever you want," he said to the animals. "Run free and have families."

"You too, Noah," said God. "You and your family must fill the earth with good people."

God put a rainbow in the sky. It stretched out in dazzling shad
from bright red to bold yellow to gentle violet.

"It means I'll never flood the Earth again," God said.

# Joseph and his Amazing Coat

Joseph lived long ago in the land of Canaan.
His father, Jacob, had many sons.

But he loved Joseph most of all. Joseph had an
amazing skill. He could tell exactly what dreams meant.

One day, Jacob bought Joseph a beautiful coat.
It was yellow and red and pink and blue and green
and every other shade under the sun.

Joseph's brothers were furious
with jealousy. They hated Joseph.

The brothers
wanted revenge.

"Let's kill him," said one.

"No," said another.
"I have a better plan."

The brothers tore
Joseph's coat and
smeared it with blood.

When they showed it to
their father, Jacob wept.

"Joseph is dead!" he cried.

The brothers sold Joseph as a slave. He was taken to Egypt and sold to a very important man named Potiphar.

Potiphar was not a cruel man, but he had a wife who was wicked and sly. She loved to make trouble.

31

One morning, she called out to her husband.

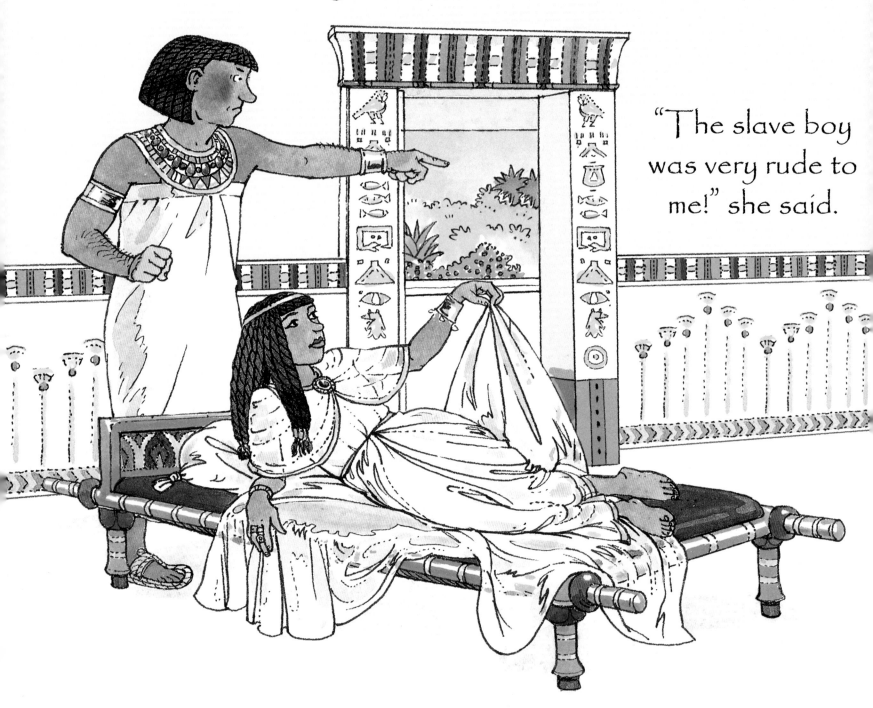

"The slave boy was very rude to me!" she said.

Potiphar went red with fury. "Guards!" he cried. "Take him away to the King's dungeons!"

The guards grabbed Joseph.

They dragged him off to the King's palace
and locked him in a lonely, dirty prison cell.

That night, the King of Egypt had a very strange dream. He saw seven fat cows and seven thin cows climb out of the Nile.

"What on earth does it mean?" he asked the next morning.

Even the wisest men in the palace had no idea.

"But we've heard that a boy called Joseph can read dreams," they said.

"Bring this Joseph here to me!" barked the King.

The palace guards looked high and low for Joseph...

until they found him in the dungeons.

Joseph was freed and taken
to the King. "I had the strangest dream,"
he said, and told Joseph all about it.

"What does it mean?" asked the King.
Joseph replied, "It means you'll have good harvests
for seven years. But then, the next seven harvests will be bad."

Sure enough, for the next seven years, the harvests were good.

There was plenty to eat and plenty to spare. Joseph made sure that the farmers stored lots of food.

So, when the bad years came, everyone in Egypt had more than enough to eat. (Thanks to Joseph.)

People came from
countries far and wide
to beg the King for food.

One day, Joseph's brothers
came to the palace, all the
way from Canaan.

When they saw Joseph, in all his
fine clothes, they thought he must
be a prince.

The brothers were given sacks full of grain. But, just before they left, the palace guards stopped them.

"Look!" said one. He held up a golden cup. "I found it in his sack!" he said. He pointed at the youngest brother, Benjamin.

"Thief!" cried the other guards. They grabbed Benjamin by the arms.

"I didn't do it!" Benjamin cried.

The guards took poor Benjamin into the palace. He stood before Joseph, trembling like a leaf.

"You stole a precious golden cup," said Joseph. He had a strange twinkle in his eye. "You will be punished!"

"Don't take our little brother!" the other brothers cried. "Punish us instead!"

"They've changed," thought Joseph with a smile. "They have passed my test. They're not cruel and heartless any more."

"Benjamin is free to go," said Joseph.
"My brother is innocent," he added.
"I put the cup into his sack myself."

"B...b...b...rother?" said Benjamin. He
peered at Joseph. His mouth fell open.

46

"It's you!" cried Benjamin.
        "It's Joseph!" cried the other brothers.

"Yes, it's me," said Joseph. They clustered around him and begged him for forgiveness. Joseph laughed and held out his arms. "Of course, I forgive you all."

# Moses in the Bulrushes

Little baby Moses was born in Egypt long, long ago.

He lived with his family beside the flowing Nile.

His parents weren't Egyptians.
They were Hebrews.

The Egyptians made the Hebrews work like slaves.
They sweated all day long in the baking sun.

The wicked King of Egypt was afraid that the
Hebrews would cause trouble one day.

"Kill all the baby Hebrew boys!" he told his guards.
"Then they'll never, ever be a threat."

The King's soldiers began their terrible task.

"I'll hide you away," said Moses' mother.

The soldiers' feet came tramping closer and closer...

She rushed to the Nile with Moses in her arms...

and quickly wove a basket out of reeds.
"You can escape along the river," she whispered.

Ever so gently, she placed Moses in the basket.

"Goodbye, my son," she whispered and
let Moses float away in the flowing water.

Moses' sister ran along the bank...

following the basket as it
sailed along the river like a tiny boat.

The water rocked Moses to sleep in his basket.

Soon, he reached a royal palace.
A princess was splashing around with her maids.

"What's that?" she cried. She'd spotted the basket.

One of her maids lifted Moses from the water.
"It's a baby, your highness!" she gasped.

The princess frowned. "Why would a mother let her baby float away?"

Then she realized, "He must be a Hebrew boy," she said. "He's escaped the soldiers!"

"I'll keep him safe," the princess said.

Just then, up ran Moses' sister.
"Would you like a nurse for the baby?" she panted.

The princess nodded,
    and the girl ran home to get her mother.

"Look after this baby," said the princess. "My father must never know that he's a Hebrew."

"I will protect him as if he was my son," said Moses' mother, with a smile.

So Moses went back to his mother
and father. He grew up safe and
strong at home.

But he couldn't stay forever. When he was older, the princess sent for him again.

"You're a prince now," said the princess.
"And the palace is your home."

68

Moses had servants to wait on him hand and foot,
    and the finest clothes and the most delicious food.

But he never forgot he was a Hebrew.

# David and Goliath

David was a shepherd boy.
He lived long ago in the land of Israel.

BAAA

Each long, hot day, he watched his father's sheep.

BAAA

He sat all alone but he wasn't lonely.
God was always by his side.

Armed with just a leather sling for throwing stones, David defended his father's sheep...

...from **roaring** lions and **growling** bears.

GRRROAR!

He knew that God would always keep him safe.

David's brothers were soldiers in King
Saul's army. One day, he took them lunch
at their army camp, nearby.

King Saul was the ruler of all Israel, and his army was huge. David had never seen so many people all in one place.

As they ate, a cry went up,

"The enemy is coming!"

The enemy army was enormous
but David wasn't afraid.

A whisper rushed through
King Saul's army:
"He's coming! He's coming!"

"Who's coming?" David asked.

He soon got an answer. Thundering
footsteps shook the earth...

THUD!

THUMP!

THUD!

David rushed to King Saul's side.
"Let me fight Goliath," he begged.

"But you're just a boy," said the King.
"And he's a giant!"

"I can do it," said
David. "God will
keep me safe."

The King agreed with a heavy sigh. He gave David his own helmet and a shiny breastplate to wear.

They were far too big.

David took off the heavy things.
"All I need are a few stones from the river," he said.

"These will do!"

He popped some stones in his bag and crossed the river to face the great Goliath.

The giant roared with laughter. "I'll finish you off in five seconds flat!" he crowed.

"HAHAHAHA!"

"No you won't," said David. "God will keep me safe."

With that, David swung his sling.
A stone flew through the air.

Whooooooooooooooooooooooooooooosh!!

It hit Goliath slap bang in the middle of his forehead.

The giant fell to the ground with a

THUMP!

He was dead. The tiny stone had killed him.

King Saul's army charged.
Their enemies ran.

"You did it, David!" said King Saul.
"I told you God would keep me safe," David replied.

The people of Israel danced and sang
when they heard about David's victory.

"How can we ever thank you?" asked the King.

"Thank God instead,"
said David. "I just threw a little stone."

# Daniel and the Lions

Daniel lived in the city of Jerusalem,
until one day, enemy soldiers invaded.

Daniel was taken to a city far, far away called Babylon.

But soon it felt as though he'd lived there all his life.

He went to school each day and
said his prayers to God each night.

As the years went by, Daniel grew into a wise young man. Even the King asked him for advice.

"You called, sire?"

The King had very vivid dreams, and Daniel always seemed to know just what they meant.

Soon, Daniel became the King's right-hand man.

Everyone had to do what he said
(except the King, of course).

The other men who worked for the King were terribly jealous of Daniel. They wanted to get rid of him. The trouble was...

...he never did anything wrong. But they noticed he prayed to God each day. This gave them a cunning idea.

Two of them went to see the King. "You are so great and mighty, my Lord," they said, in soft voices.

"People should bow down to you, and only you," they said.

"It should be against the law to worship anyone else."

101

The King made the law without
thinking very much about it.

He forgot that Daniel always
prayed to God three times a day.

One evening, Daniel's enemies
spied on him from behind a clump of trees.

He was kneeling beside his window, praying.
They ran as fast as they could to tell the King.

The King was heartbroken. He was very fond of Daniel. But the law was the law.

Daniel had to be punished for his crime.

Soldiers flung him in a pit full of ravenous lions.

GROAAAR!

RAAAAH!

RAAAAAH!

"May your God protect you," cried the King.

105

The King walked sadly home.

He couldn't eat. He couldn't sleep. He kept worrying about Daniel in the pit.

Early the next morning, he walked ever so slowly to the edge of the pit. He could hardly bear to look inside.

"Did your God save you?" he cried.
Then he looked, but could not see Daniel anywhere.

Daniel was sitting up against the wall.
The lions were dozing like kittens.

"God stopped the lions from killing me," he said.

The King was thrilled.

He called to his guards,
"Let Daniel out of there!"

"Throw those traitors in
the pit instead," he added.

Daniel's enemies were shoved down into the pit.

The lions were waiting, hungrily.

The King and Daniel walked in the palace garden as the sun sank low. "You were right all along," said the King.

"From now on, everyone must pray to your God."

"Even you?" asked Daniel.

"Especially me," the King replied.

# Jonah and the Whale

Long ago, when the world was very young, a man named Jonah lived in Israel.

He loved his home, where the sun shone brightly...

...the birds tweeted gently

...and the sheep
bleated softly.

Jonah prayed to God each day to thank him for all this.

One night, God spoke to Jonah.
"I have a job for you," he said.

Jonah almost jumped out of his skin.
He trembled from head to toe and back again.

"You must go to Nineveh!"

"The people there are very wicked. Tell them to change their ways," God added. "Or I will destroy them."

Jonah didn't want to go. He was scared of the people in Nineveh. But he was scared of God too.

"I'll run away to sea," he thought. "I'll go so far that even God won't see me."

He set off for the port to find a ship to carry him across the sea.

At the port, he found a ship
that was just about to sail away.
"Take me with you," he begged the captain.

The captain agreed and they set sail.
But a storm began to rise on the horizon.

Soon, the boat was lashed by mighty waves. The terrible storm began to toss and batter and hurl the boat around.

The sailors were terrified.

But Jonah stayed sound asleep until
the captain shook him wide awake.

"Ask your God to save us," the captain begged.
"I can't," said Jonah. "If I pray, he'll see me."

But Jonah knew it was his fault. "The storm is God's anger," he said. "If you throw me in the sea, the water will be calm again."

The captain said, "I can't do that!"
"But we can!" said the sailors. So they
heaved Jonah up into the air and threw him...

SPLASH!
into the sea.

Jonah sank
down
and down beneath the waves.

And into the mouth
of a gigantic whale.

Jonah coughed and spluttered and blinked.
"I'm still alive," he thought.

He was sitting in the slimy belly of the whale.

Jonah lived inside the whale for three whole days.

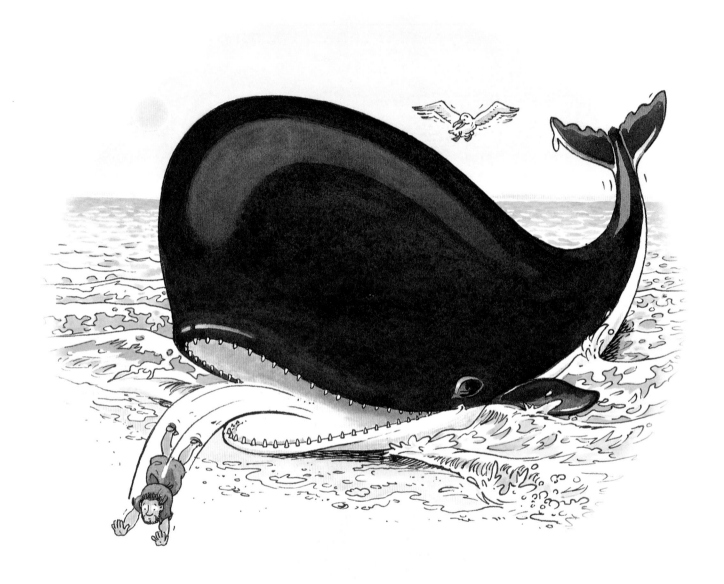

Then, with a cough like thunder, the whale spat him out onto a beach.

"Hello Jonah," said God. "It's time to go to Nineveh."

"You're almost there."

This time, Jonah did as he was told. He hurried off to Nineveh to tell the people to change their ways.

In Nineveh, he went to see the King.
"Tell your people to stop being wicked," he said.

"Or God will destroy your city." The King went pale.
"You must go without food and water to show you're sorry!" he told his people.

The people did as they were told. They didn't eat or drink, and they prayed to God. Jonah walked up onto a hill to watch and wait.

Night fell, but the city was still safe and sound.

"I have spared them," God told Jonah. "They're not wicked any more."

Jonah was angry. "Why did you forgive them?" he asked God. "They're wicked and cruel!"

"Because I am merciful," said God.

"I am everywhere."

"And I love everyone."

# About these stories

All these stories come from the Bible, which was written thousands of years ago. The Bible is split up into lots of different sections, or books, which are divided into chapters. Here's where the stories in this book appear in the Bible:

**Noah's Ark**
The story of Noah's Ark comes from the very first book in the Bible, which is known as Genesis. Noah's story starts in Chapter 6 of Genesis.

**Joseph and his Amazing Coat**
You'll also find the story of Joseph in Genesis. It starts in Chapter 37.

**Moses in the Bulrushes**
There are lots of stories about Moses in the book known as Exodus. The stories about him as a baby start in Chapter 1.

**David and Goliath**
The story of David and Goliath is in the book known as Samuel 1, and it starts in Chapter 17.

**Daniel and the Lions**
There's a whole book named after Daniel, and the story of his journey to Babylon as a little boy begins in Chapter 1.

**Jonah and the Whale**
There's also a book named after Jonah. It's very short, and the story of Jonah and the Whale takes up the whole book.

Based on adaptations by Heather Amery; Edited by Jenny Tyler and Jane Chisholm
Additional designs by Emily Bornoff and Maria Wheatley; Additional illustrations by Candice Whatmore
Cover design by Russell Punter and Caroline Spatz; Digital manipulation by Nick Wakeford and John Russell
Biblical consultant: Bridget O'Brien; With thanks to Benjamin Morse